It all happened just before the first Christmas night of all Christmas nights...

NATIVITY STORIES

Alan Howard

Illustrations by
Leszek Forczek

DAWNE-LEIGH PUBLICATIONS   SAN RAFAEL, CALIFORNIA

Copyright © 1980 by Alan Howard

Dawne-Leigh Publications
231 Adrian Road
Millbrae, CA 94030

Distributed by Atheneum Publishers
Vreeland Avenue
Boro of Totowa
Paterson, N.J. 07512

Manufactured in the United States of America

Library of Congress Cataloging in Publication Data

Howard, Alan
    Nativity stories.

        SUMMARY: Presents six stories about the birth of Jesus.
        1.   Jesus Christ—Nativity—Juvenile fiction.   2. Christmas stories. [1.   Jesus
Christ—Nativity—Fiction.   2. Christmas   stories.   3. Short   stories]   I.   Forczek,
Leszek, 1946–
II.   Title.
PZ7.H83225Nat   [Fic]   79-20746
ISBN 0-89742-027-6

Contents

_____ Part I _____

Foreword

"TELL US A STORY"

The stories in this book arose in connection with the celebration of Advent at Michael House Waldorf School in Derbyshire, England. It was the custom every year on the first day of Advent to bring the children in to the school hall, which was decorated with Christmas greenery and flowers and was illuminated by numerous candles. In the center of the hall, hanging from the ceiling, was a large Advent sphere, a wire construction covered with greenery and made according to Celtic origin in twelve segments with twelve candles placed at equal distances around the circumference. The children came into the hall to the soft strains of Christmas music; and when they were comfortably seated under and around the sphere, it was the custom for one of the teachers to tell a story bearing on Advent.

For several years that privilege fell to me; and a more inspiring atmosphere in which to tell a story, touching on this most exciting season of the year, can not be imagined. The hundred or so children, their eyes shining in the candlelight, only needed the opening words to spirit them away to that magic land of imagination where all stories have their origin.

The problem, of course, was a suitable story. It had to be one that deepened the mood and meaning of Advent — that anticipation and preparation for the Christ child, whose birth in a stable is celebrated on Christmas night. The preparation and reception of the children in the beautiful candlelit hall, as well as their own expectancy at the proximity of Christmas, had already done much to achieve that. I felt that it was my job to try and intensify the magnitude of the event by linking it with the familiar, so that it would have meaning for the youngest child there.

That meant — for me at any rate — "making up" a story.

Now in "making up" a story, particularly one connected with an historical event, there is always the problem of how far one is justified in doing so. The story is bound to be imaginary and therefore "untrue"; and it might be argued that this could be prejudicial, especially to young children, who are likely to take what an adult says, in particular, the teacher, as "gospel."

But truth is of many kinds. There is a truth of imagination, as there is of facts; and though the two might not correspond with one another, they are both none-the-less true. Even when a child asks, "Is that story true?" he or she is not necessarily asking for empirical corroboration; and the proper answer, provided the story isn't a trivial or worthless one, is yes. When they are older you will be able to differentiate between the different kinds of truth; but for the time being the child wants confirmation of what he has felt as the effect of the story. The truth of the story is what it does for you, not what it depicts; and what it does *for you either by making a better person of you, or in enhancing for you some other item of your experience or knowledge. If the story does that, then all is "grist to the mill" of the story teller in what he uses to achieve it.*

Many of the great paintings of the Middle Ages and Renaissance depict the birth of Jesus; but they often have a background in which characters and objects, incidental to the stable scene, are drawn directly from the contemporary world and life of the artist. This is obviously "untrue," but no one is disturbed by it. What makes the picture great is how powerfully the total composition impresses the mind and heart with the magnitude of the main event. If it does that, then it doesn't matter what the artist does to achieve it; indeed, his very originality or naivete in putting his theme in a setting it could not possibly have had, often does more to emphasize his point then verisimilitude.

And a story is a picture, a picture painted on the ethereal canvas of the imagination.

But there is something else.

The birth of the Jesus child is generally regarded in the Christian world as the greatest event of all time. There could have been nothing fortuitous or arbitrary about it. It had been prepared by heavenly powers since the beginning of the world, and Hebrew prophets had spoken of it, and the history of their race had intimated it since that history began.

Such an event, therefore, casts its significance over the commonest most ordinary detail associated with it, such as a stable, for instance. Stables, however, are quite commonplace, ordinary things; but the stable in which Jesus was born could have been no ordinary stable. Mangers, too, are nothing on the whole to tell a story about; but the manger in which that newborn child was laid was the manger above all other mangers.

This endowment of a special quality to things by reason of the great events and people connected with them is obvious from the importance which is still attached to sacred relics. At the time of writing, a great deal of public interest is being shown in a shroud which is purported to be the shroud in which the holy body of Christ was wrapped. Now a shroud is for all practical purposes just a piece of linen, and a piece of linen is nothing to get excited about; but when it is possibly the piece of linen in which the body of Christ was wrapped, then it becomes something which everybody pays deference to, and which acquires a value beyond price. Even we ourselves attach a significance and value to otherwise quite worthless objects, simply because they were used by, or belonged to, someone we specially revered or loved.

But if things have a value which they acquired in connection with some special event, they also have a story in themselves as to how they came into that position. They were made, or used, or owned by some human being or other before they were linked with the great event or figure with which they were subsequently associated. They didn't just happen to be there. Someone was instrumental in their being there.

It was this link between the incidental and the outstanding that I wanted to bring out; and it was the "someone" connected with the details of the stable, the manger and so on in the birth of Jesus scene, that I allowed my imagination to play on. Although what I have said about them has no foundation in fact, in so far as it reflects the radiance or importance of the main event, then it is true. It is not only the historical truth of the birth of Jesus I have sought to indicate in these stories, but the implicit truth, that this event was known and was prepared for by powers in heaven and on earth; a truth which we still recognize in that we celebrate such a season as Advent at all—"for this thing was not done in a corner."

And so these stories arose and were told in successive years in the circumstances I have described.

Before leaving them, however, there is one other thing I would like to say about them. These stories were told and retold without any previous writing down. There is all the difference in the world between telling a story and reading one from one's own or another's composition. Whether a story is read or told it will accomplish its task of stimulating the imagination and the feelings; but when you tell it something happens to it between you and the listener which can never be recaptured in writing. The story itself takes part in the telling, and you become the listener as well as the teller; for you have entered that magic land of imagination which exists somewhere between the sound of your voice, and the light of your listener's eyes.

Every one of us—of the older generation, at least, for alas! the telling of stories to children is so much out of fashion these days—must have treasured memories of a parent or a beloved relative telling us stories when we were children; and those experiences still live vividly in the memory, enshrined in a warmth of human intimacy which none of the harsher experiences we may have met since can ever eradicate.

So, whenever a child comes to you with the age-old request, "Tell me a story, please," do just that. Tell one. Don't immediately look around for a book to read from—not even this book. Refuse to ease your conscience by saying how much better the writer's version is than yours could possibly be; and suppress the cowardly weakness that wants to say, "I'm no good at telling stories." You don't know how good you are till you try; and you can't possibly know what you're missing until you do.

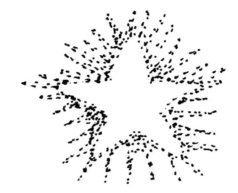

———————————— Part II ————————————

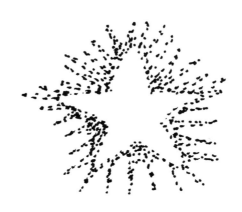

THE STABLE

THE STABLE

It all happened just before the first Christmas night of all Christmas nights, and that, as you know, was a long, long time ago. And it happened to Benjamin, a boy who lived with his father in an inn on the edge of the little town of Bethlehem, just beside the road that runs from Bethlehem to the great city of Jerusalem.

Benjamin's father was the innkeeper; and as people were constantly going by, he was able to earn enough to keep both himself and his son. Benjamin, of course, used to help his father. He quite liked the life of the inn, meeting all the people from different parts of the country and listening to their conversations and their stories. Apart from that, however, nothing very exciting or wonderful ever happened at the inn. Nobody very great or important ever passed the night there as they did at other inns along the road, the bigger and better ones; for the one belonging to his father was not good enough for them. Sometimes Benjamin caught a glimpse of these great people as they passed by, but they never stopped. Camel drivers, merchants, messengers on their way to and fro were all who came to them. So, when Benjamin's father said one day, "We must get ready for the taxing; there will be a lot of people coming by when that starts," Benjamin wondered whether things might change. This taxing, his father spoke of, happened because the king wanted money for all the things he had to do; and so he sent out messengers to all the towns and villages round about, to tell the people that they must come to Jerusalem by a certain date and pay their taxes.

"I think we should clean out that old stable," Benjamin's father said. "You never know, we may have need of it when the crowds start coming."

This stable, however, was really nothing but an old shed behind the inn, built in front of a cave in the rocky hillside. Benjamin could not even remember when it was last used, and he could not imagine why his father thought it would be needed now. But if his father wanted it cleaned, cleaned it should be.

So, the next day Benjamin went to work. What a job he had! The stable was in a shocking state. There was dirt everywhere, but he set to with a will. After working all the morning, he managed to get the worst of the mess out, and the floor reasonably clean.

As he was resting on his brush, looking at what he had done and thinking that he had made a pretty good job of it, he was surprised to hear a voice behind him saying, "I do not think it is good enough yet; considerably more will have to be done before it is really ready." Turning round, Benjamin found someone who was a complete stranger to him—standing just inside the door and looking around everywhere with the most critical eye. "No, it certainly will not do yet," the stranger concluded.

"Won't do for what?" Benjamin exclaimed, for he was just a little annoyed to think that anybody but his father should complain about his work.

But the words were hardly out of his mouth, when, to his surprise, the stranger was not there any more. He had gone, vanished, just like that. Benjamin did not even see him go like you would see anybody else go. The stranger just disappeared.

Benjamin could hardly believe his eyes and, wondering whether he was dreaming, just stood for a moment staring at the spot where the stranger had been.

"People don't just disappear like that," he said to himself and, realizing that the stranger could not have gone far, he dashed outside still clutching his brush, hoping to catch sight of him. He looked everywhere up and down the road, and although he could see for a long way in both directions, t.iere was not a sign of the stranger anywhere.

Well, you can imagine that gave Benjamin something to think about. He just did not know what to make of it. When he got back to the stable he found himself looking around just like the stranger had done. It was quite true; the stable was still very, very dirty. The floor was clean enough—for a stable that is—but the walls were covered with dirt; and as for the ceiling, great dusty cobwebs hung down almost to the floor in some places.

He was on the point of going to ask his father whether he had sent the stranger, or whether he knew anything about him. But his father had gone out to see a neighbor, and Benjamin decided on second thought that he would not say anything to his father yet. He would do some more work on the stable the next day and would see if the stranger returned.

So, the next morning he began to work again, making the walls the chief object of his attentions. That meant, of course, that he had to do yesterday's work all over again, for the dirt came down off the walls all over the floor. However, he did not mind. He kept at it, and presently it was finished. "Now," he thought to himself, "if that stranger comes again, I'll be ready for him."

But he was not ready; for even as he was thinking about it, there was the stranger, just inside the door, looking around everywhere just as he had done before.

"No," he said at length, after he had looked it all over; "it still will not do. It is better, but it is not fit for the King yet."

"The King!" exclaimed Benjamin, but once again, before he could even get the words out, the stranger was gone. Though Benjamin dashed out after him, running some way up and down the road this time, he could not catch sight of him anywhere.

Well by now his curiosity was really aroused. What would a king want that old stable for? And what kind of a king could he be? Kings had to do with palaces, not stables. They left all that to their servants. But the stranger had distinctly said "King." It was more mysterious than ever.

Now Benjamin remembered that he had not told his father anything about what had happened; and although he thought that perhaps he ought to do so, he decided after all that he would still keep it a secret and see what happened. He would go on working at that stable until it was impossible for anyone to complain about the slightest thing. "Then," he said to himself, "I might find out what it's all about."

So the next day, and for many days after that, whenever he had some time to spare, he was in the stable, cleaning away wherever he found the tiniest bit of dirt. And every day when he had finished, there was the stranger, looking around as before; and although he always noticed what improvements had been made and appreciated them, he always seemed to find something that was still not good enough.

But an end had to come sometime, and so indeed it did. One day the stranger, after looking round everywhere, turned to Benjamin with a smile on his face such as Benjamin had never seen on the face of a human being and said, "Yes, I think it will do now. As it has to be a stable and not a palace, there can not be a cleaner stable anywhere in the whole world." And with that he was gone.

Now while all this had been going on, every day more and

more people had been coming along the road to Jerusalem for the taxing. Every night they crowded into the inn for rest and shelter. At last there came a night—it was a night that people would remember ever after as the most wonderful night since the world began—when the inn was full to the door. People were sleeping everywhere, on the floor, the tables, the chairs, wherever they could find a space; for people did not mind where they slept in those days, as long as they had a roof over their heads.

The innkeeper had gone to stand by his front door, to tell anyone else who might come that way that there was no room for them. But just as he was thinking that he could at last shut up for the night, he saw an old man leaning on a staff, making his way slowly toward him. The innkeeper could see he was hoping to find lodging there, so he hurried forward to tell him it was no good coming any further.

"I'm sorry," he said, " if you're looking for lodging here, you're unlucky. My inn is already full."

The old man stopped and, after looking at the innkeeper for a moment as though he could not believe his ears, retraced his steps. The innkeeper could see, in the shadows, a young woman sitting on a donkey. "It's no good, Mary," he heard the old man say, "there's no room here either. We shall have to go on further still."

"Oh Joseph!" the woman cried, and the cry pierced the innkeeper's heart, "whatever shall we do? I must rest somewhere this night of all nights."

The innkeeper was so moved by her distress that in spite of all he had said, he began to wonder whether he really could put them up somewhere. And then — "Just," as he said afterwards, "as if somebody had whispered it in my ear," —he suddenly thought of the old stable.

Running quickly to them, he said, "I've just remembered something. I can give you lodging after all. There isn't any room in the inn, it's true. However, if you're not too particular, I've got a stable you can have, and you can have it all to yourselves. It's beautifully clean. My boy has hardly been doing anything else but cleaning it for days." And fetching a lantern, he led them, donkey and all, into the stable at the side of the inn.

"There," he said as he flung open the door, "you can stay here, and no one will disturb you." After waiting to see them comfortably settled, he shut the door, went back to his own bed, and fell fast asleep.

It was sometime later when Benjamin, who had gone to bed as tired as his father, woke up and, for some strange reason, could not go back to sleep again. He was wide awake. As it was still some hours before morning, he got up and stood by his little window, looking out at the night.

It was a beautiful night. The village, the hills, and the fields all around seemed bathed in a deep heavenly peace. He had never known such a night, and he felt as if he were the only one awake in the whole sleeping world around him.

Then his heart seemed to stop beating. He happened to be looking toward the stable, wondering why in spite of all the work he had done, and in spite of all the mysterious things the stranger had said, nothing seemed to have happened about it. At that instant, he noticed a great shining light streaming out from underneath the door and through the cracks in the woodwork.

He could imagine only one cause for it.

"My stable," he cried, "it must be on fire!" Without another thought he pulled on some clothes and dashed out. He was there in a moment or two and, pulling open the doors, prepared himself for the first burst of flame, when, to his amazement, he saw, not the fire he had expected, but a newborn baby from whom all this wonderful light shone. It was lying peacefully asleep in the manger, and a beautiful lady in a blue gown was smiling down on him, while an old man leaning on his staff watched over them both. But what a baby and what a mother, and father too. There had never been in all the world a family quite like that.

Somehow Benjamin knew that this must be the King of whom the stranger had spoken. How he knew he could not have said; but because he knew, he knelt down before them and bowed his head in reverence.

Presently, as he knelt there he heard a voice speaking to him, and a thrill ran through him as he listened. For it was a voice he knew, a voice he had heard before, and it was speaking to him and was calling him by name.

"Benjamin," he heard it say, "look up and be the first in all the world to behold that child who is to be King of all mankind. In the years to come many men will build wonderful temples to his memory; but you, and you alone, without knowing what you did, have prepared his first home on Earth."

Slowly, very slowly, as if he were almost afraid to look at the stranger,who he now realized was an angel of God, in the face again, he raised his eyes and saw once again how the whole stable was transfigured with heavenly light. It was indeed a palace, and the little family within it was indeed a royal family, beyond all royalty that ever was on Earth.

And finally, still half afraid to do so, he looked the stranger full in the face and saw there an angel of God, clothed in light, and with mighty wings outspread, enfolding Mary and Joseph and the Child Jesus. Suddenly the whole air was filled with music and singing. The roof of the stable seemed to disappear, and countless other angels, rank on rank, reaching up to the very heavens and ascending and descending round the heads of those gathered there, sang together, "Glory to God in the Highest, and on Earth, Peace to Men of Good Will."

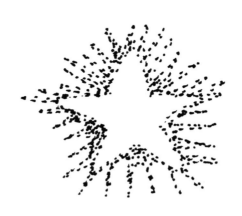

THE MANGER

THE MANGER

In the little town of Bethlehem at the time when Jesus was born, there lived an old carpenter named Reuben and his wife Sarah. He was not the only carpenter in Bethlehem, but he was certainly the best. Yet in spite of that, at the time our story took place, nobody seemed to have anything for him to do.

He had not done any work for days, and there did not seem any likelihood of his doing anything in the future, either. He had never known such a time. And so he had been sitting all day in his workshop wondering what was going to happen to him, while his poor wife was sitting in the house wondering what they were going to have for supper, and where it was going to come from, for there was nothing at all left in her cupboard.

As old people's thoughts do, Reuben's turned to earlier, happier times when things went very much better. He had had a very good friend then with whom he had worked, a young man named Joseph.

Reuben had hoped at one time that he and Joseph might set up a workshop together, but Joseph had had other ideas. "I don't want to stay here all my life," he had said. "I want to see a bit of the world." It was not long before Joseph had left Bethlehem for good, and Reuben had never seen or heard of him again.

"I wonder what he's doing now," he pondered. "I certainly hope that he's doing better than I am"; for as things were now, Reuben would not have wanted anyone else to share them with him.

But as he was thinking about all this something made him look up, and to his surprize he saw that a stranger had come into his workshop. He was standing there by the bench looking round as if he were trying to decide what sort of a carpenter's shop it was. How long he might have been there Reuben could not say, for he had not heard him come in; but in the hope that he was at last going to get something to do, he got up quickly to attend to him.

"Could you make me a manger?" the stranger asked.

"Why -er, yes, of course," said Reuben. He had made dozens of mangers in his time, and there was nothing unusual about that; but he could not help wondering what such a stranger could want with a manger. He was not like any of the people who lived round about, and they were the only kind of people who ever wanted mangers made. Reuben wondered what part of the country he came from, too. He looked as though he were a very important person.

He was just about to ask him what kind of manger he wanted,

when the stranger went on to explain in detail how it had to be made. Although it was nothing more than the ordinary kind of manger, the stranger was nonetheless very particular about it. "I want it very well made," he said, "and beautifully finished." This struck Reuben as very unusual. People were not usually bothered about the finish of things like mangers. As long as they were strongly made and would stand up to rough wear, they were generally satisfied. "I don't want anything rough or unplaned, " the stranger added. "It should be as smooth and beautiful as a bed for a king."

While Reuben was wondering just what sort of a customer he had to deal with, the stranger walked over to the planks of wood standing in the corner. He very carefully chose the best piece among them and said, "I would like it made out of this"; and he ran his finger across it just like someone stroking a very valuable work of art. "I don't know how much it will cost," he said, "but I expect this will be enough"; and laying a coin on the bench, he added, "If it is any more, I will pay you when I see you again"; and without another word he left the shop.

When Reuben told his wife about it afterwards, there was one thing he could not understand. He could not remember seeing the stranger go. He had gone of course, but Reuben could not for the life of him remember seeing him do so. He just seemed to disappear. One moment he was there, telling Reuben what kind of manger to make, and the next he was gone.

But Reuben was too excited to bother about that now, for there was certainly no question about the stranger having been there. There on the bench was a real shining piece of silver, real silver; and what was more, enough to make several mangers and still have something left over.

With an exclamation of joy he had rushed in to tell his wife the good news; and while she went out to buy something for supper, he began straight away cutting out the pieces to make it.

And what a manger it was when it was finished!

I told you Reuben was a good carpenter; but never in all his life had his eye been so true, or his hand so steady, as he sawed and planed the wood to make this manger. It was a real master-piece—really too good for cattle to eat out of. He looked forward with pride to the return of the stranger, who he knew would be as pleased with it as he was.

But day after day went by and the stranger never came to fetch it. Reuben looked for him each day; for he had carefully put aside the exact change from the silver piece, so that he would be able to give it to him when he came, but still he did not come.

Something else happened, however, which Reuben only understood later when he found out who the stranger really was; for as soon as the manger was finished it seemed as if everybody in Bethlehem suddenly wanted Reuben to make something for them. He had never in his life been so busy; and as he had plenty of money now to buy the wood he needed, he was able to satisfy them all. From morning to night working away at his bench, he was one of the happiest men in all Bethlehem.

But still the stranger did not come. The manger stood there in the corner of his workshop unclaimed day after day. The change from the silver piece lay untouched in a little bowl on a high shelf.

One day, however, Isaac, the innkeeper, who kept an inn on the edge of town nearest to Jerusalem, dropped in to see his friend and neighbor Reuben. The moment he got inside the door he saw the manger and immediately wanted to buy it.

"D'you know, Reuben," he explained, going over to where the manger stood and running his fingers over its smooth surface, "it's a strange thing, but you might have made that very manger for me. You know that old stable of mine—well, I suddenly decided the other day to have it cleaned out. It hasn't been used for years; and my boy Benjamin has made such a fine job of it, that I decided to get a manger for it. And here you have the very thing. How much d'you want for it?"

"I'm afraid it isn't for sale," replied Reuben; and seeing the disappointment on Isaac's face, he told him the story of the stranger, and how he was still waiting for him to fetch it. "So you see I can't sell it to you; it's already sold."

But Isaac was one of those men who, once they have their heart set on something, are not to be put off so easily. "All right," he said, "then make me another one like it; only remember it must be just like it, so like it that you won't be able to tell them apart."

"I'll see what I can do," Reuben said; and as soon as Isaac was gone, he chose a piece of wood and set to work.

But now another difficulty arose; one that could have made a good carpenter like Reuben feel thoroughly ashamed of himself. He could not make another one. He, Reuben, the best carpenter in Bethlehem, could not make another manger. He tried, but he made so many mistakes with it, that in the end he had to scrap everything and start again. And the second try was no better than the first. He could not understand it. It seemed as though there were some kind of spell on him. Either he cut his pieces too short, or the wood split just as he was finishing it off, or the grain was all against him. Nothing seemed to go right. He decided to try just once more, but the same thing happened, and in the end he gave up trying altogether; for, of course, he had other things to do which could not wait—though, strangely enough, nothing went wrong with any of those.

When Isaac called to collect his manger, Reuben had to tell him what had happened; and when Issac had heard the whole story, he was as puzzled as Reuben. The two of them just stood there for some time looking at each other without a word.

Presently Isaac's face lit up, as a brilliant idea came to him. "I know what we can do," he said. "Let me put this manger you have made in my stable for the time being. After all, it's getting pretty crowded here. Then, if the stranger comes to fetch it, you will only have to run around to my place, and he can have it. Besides, " he added, "when he has taken it away, perhaps everything will be all right again, and you'll be able to make one for me without any mistakes."

But Reuben did not like this idea at all. He not only thought of what might happen to his beautiful manger—for there was not a scratch on it now—but he could not help wondering whether the stranger was putting him to some kind of test; and that if he let the manger go, the stranger would have cause for complaint. He was bound to come back, if only for his change, and if the manger was not there, what would he say? "No, I couldn't possibly do that," Reuben declared.

By now, however, Isaac was as determined to have the manger as Reuben was not to let go, and they must have argued for a full hour before Reuben finally agreed. Even then Reuben made Isaac solemnly promise to take good care of it.

"Don't worry," said Isaac, as he triumphantly picked it up to carry it away. "I'll take as much care of it as if I'd made it myself; and what's more you can come along every day, two or three times a day if you like, and if there's so much as a speck of dust on it, you can take it right back again."

So off went Isaac with the manger, and Reuben returned to his bench, half expecting every minute to see the stranger standing there demanding, "Where's that manger you promised to make for me?" But he did not come, neither that day nor the next, and in the end so many days went by that Reuben began to think he would never see him again, and that Isaac could have the manger after all.

Now all the time this was going on, more and more people were making their way through Bethlehem to Jerusalem, where they had to go at that time to pay their taxes to the king; and there came a night when so many were staying there that every inn and even every house where there was any room to spare was full.

Reuben and his wife had gone to bed early that night, and they had been sound asleep for several hours when they were awakened by the noise of singing out in the street. At first Reuben thought it was some drunken revellers going home; but when he went to the window, he saw three shepherds whom he knew very well, and who were usually out on the hills at that time of night looking after their flocks.

"What in the world are you doing down there making all that noise?" he called out to them. "Don't you know that everybody is asleep, or trying to sleep?"

At these words the shepherds stopped and looked up to see where the voice was coming from. One of them recognized Reuben. "Oh, Reuben," he cried, "This is no time for sleeping, even if it is night. The most wonderful thing in the world has happened; and here in our village too. The Messiah, the Saviour, was born this night, and in a place you'd never guess—in Isaac's stable, just down the road." Thereupon he proceeded to tell him how they had all been looking after their sheep on the hills, when an angel came and told them all about it and bade them go and greet the child; and how the heavens were suddenly filled with angels singing "Glory to God"; and how, leaving their flocks, they came straightway and saw that it was indeed so. "We poor shepherds, not the king, nor the Roman governor, not even the priests," he added with great pride, "are the first to have seen this Holy Child. So come on down, and let us show you. You mustn't sleep any more on a night like this; come down and go with us to the stable."

Reuben still felt sure that they had been drinking, but he put on some clothes and came down. Quite apart from what they had been

40

telling him, the fact that it was something to do with Isaac's stable had reminded him of his manger; and he wanted to make sure that that was all right.

As they went along the shepherds told him more details of all that had happened; but they kept interrupting each other so much, that he was still unable to make much sense out of it all, until they got to the stable.

Then he had no doubt. There, indeed, before him was the Child with its mother and father, and behind them stood an angel of God, clothed in light which filled the whole place and shone out even into the road and the fields beyond.

But now a great fear came over Reuben; for, as he looked, he saw that the face of the angel was exactly the same as the face of the stranger who had come into his workshop so many weeks before and had asked him to make a manger. A manger? Of course, in the wonder of what was before him he had forgotten that for a moment, but now looking down he saw that the Holy Child was lying asleep on some straw in the very manger that he himself had made.

Suddenly he realized what it all meant. That was why the angel had not come to fetch the manger; why, too, Isaac had had to have it in his stable so that it should be there when this took place; and particularly why the stranger had said he had wanted it to be fit for the bed of a king. This Child, of course, was the King he had meant.

So, not knowing what else to do, Reuben pulled off his cap and sank on his knees before the Child, remaining there with his head bowed, not daring to look any more. But presently he heard a voice speaking to him and calling him by name. It was a voice he knew; for had he not heard it many weeks before in his own workshop when the angel, who was now looking after this holy family, had come to him there.

"Look up, Reuben, thou faithful servant of God," the angel was saying; "have no fear of all these wonderful things that have come to pass; for thou thyself art one chosen by God to help bring them to pass."

And as Reuben slowly raised his eyes in obedience to the angel's command, he looked again upon the Holy Child as it lay sleeping in the manger, and the mother, the beautiful young woman clothed in red and blue who sat there watching her child. Presently he let his glance travel to where the father an elderly man dressed in a brown robe stood leaning on his staff and found the father looking not at the child, or the mother, but at Reuben himself, and with a face transfigured with joy.

"Who was this?" Reuben thought. He seemed to know that face from somewhere, but he was sure that he had not seen it for a long time. And then . . . Could it possibly be . . . ? Was it really . . . his old friend . . . Joseph? Yes! There was no doubt about it. In a moment the two of them with tears of joy in their eyes were clasping each other in a fond embrace, while the angel—for 'tis said that angels smile—smiled a heavenly blessing upon them.

How much more rejoicing there was in Bethlehem that night, and how much these two old friends had to tell each other, I must leave you to imagine. Reuben only left his friend for a few moments to hurry home to tell his wife Sarah, and to bring her along to share the wonder of all that had happened.

In the days that followed, these two families were hardly ever apart for a moment. And when the time came for Joseph and Mary to go back to Nazareth, Reuben and his wife decided to go with them.

They left the manger behind. Isaac was so proud of it now, and of all that had taken place in his stable, that they could not bear to take the manger away. He kept it in the stable just as it was and would let no one touch it but himself. Anyone who came to the inn afterwards could consider themselves specially honored if, in the course of their stay, he took them out to the stable and, after unlocking the door, let them have a peek inside, while he told them about all the wonderful things that had happened that night.

What eventually happened to the manger, however, and indeed what happened to the stable itself, no one knows now; for all this happened a very long time ago. But people have never forgotten where it all happened; and even today they still go, some of them half way across the world, just to see the place where that stable was, and where that manger stood, and where he who was to be the Saviour of mankind spent his first night on Earth.

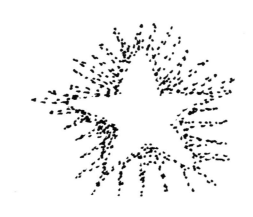

THE DONKEY

THE DONKEY

He was only a little donkey, but as strong and well formed as a donkey could be. As he tossed his head and flung up his heels, however, in the little enclosure behind Jonah's house, Jonah, his master, scowled. "You rascal," he muttered, "you ought to be bringing me the best price for a donkey in the Nazareth market that's ever been paid hereabout. Instead of that..." and he clenched his teeth in bitterness as he thought of all he had had to suffer for that one donkey.

For truth to tell it seemed the most obstinate, bad tempered donkey that ever was foaled. Neither man, woman, nor child would it allow to get on its back; and if the lightest of loads were laid there, it would hump itself up and kick and shake until, even with the strongest fastenings, the load usually ended up either on the ground or hanging under its body. Yet no one had ever seen a more beautiful donkey; and with that blue-greyish coat of the softest hair and those two artfully pointed ears, it was the admiration of all. But let anyone only just try to get on its back, and it became a fury of resistance.

It was no good beating it. People in that country and at that time (for you must remember it was a long, long time ago—just before Jesus was born in Bethlehem) were not particularly kind to donkeys anyway, and this one's master was crueller than most. He had beaten it so terribly that only the fact that it was still worth money to him—and money was very important to Jonah—had restrained him from beating it to death.

"I shall just have to sell it for what I can get," he grumbled to himself. "Let's hope there's someone at the market who will be fool enough to buy it." But his donkey being already known for its strange behavior, even that was not very likely. Of course, if Jonah had known anything about donkeys—I mean really known anything about them—he might have guessed that there was a reason why this one could behave so crossly and yet could look so sweet. But how was Jonah to know that? A donkey was just a donkey to him, and had no other purpose than to bear on his poor back whatever anyone might care to pile on it.

So the donkey's secret (and he did have a secret, a very wonderful secret of something he alone had to do) remained with him, and on the very next market day Jonah took it to the market, hoping to get rid of it for as much as possible.

Now about that time, Joseph and Mary, who also lived in Nazareth, were busy preparing for their journey to Jerusalem, where Joseph had to go with all the other people who were born in Jerusalem to pay their taxes to the king. It was not a journey Joseph was looking forward to very much, for soon Mary's child was to be born; and he could not leave her by herself at home, he would have to take her with him.

"We shall have to buy a donkey," he said; "it is impossible for you to walk with me all the way to Jerusalem." He took out the bag where he kept his money, to count over once again how much he could spare for the purchase.

"But can we afford a donkey?" Mary asked. Although Joseph earned enough by his carpentry to keep them both, extra money for things like donkeys was not easily come by.

"I think so," replied Joseph, " if they're not too dear. And perhaps the Lord will be good to us, and we shall be able to find a bargain."

So off they both went to the market and looked at all the donkeys that were there for sale. They found several which were suitable, but all of them were too dear, much too dear. Poor Joseph was almost in despair. They had to be off in a few days, and they could not go without a donkey.

"Let's have one more look around," said Mary. "Perhaps we haven't seen everything yet. There must be one which we could afford."

So off they went again, and as they turned a corner at the farthest side of the market, Mary stopped. "Look, Joseph," she said, laying her hand on his arm. "There's our donkey, I'm sure. Why didn't we see it the last time we came round?'' and in her eagerness to see it at closer quarters she began half leading, half pulling her not so enthusiastic husband to where the donkey stood.

This, of course, was Jonah's donkey; and Jonah, not wanting to put himself too much in the public eye before people had had a good chance to see the donkey, had half hidden himself behind a potter's stall. When Mary came up, seeing how interested she obviously was, he came out from where he was hiding and waited to see if they were going to buy it.

"What a beautiful donkey!'' Mary was saying, while she stroked his smooth silky coat. "I'm sure he's just the one for us, Joseph.''

"If it's not too dear like all the others,'' Joseph muttered, though even he had to admit to himself that it was best they had seen so far.

"Did you want to buy a donkey,'' Jonah asked, coming forward with a beaming smile on his face; and without waiting for them to reply to such an obvious question, he went on, "You're in luck, if you do. You won't find a donkey like this anywhere.''

Joseph looked at it for a long time, walking all round it to examine it from every angle. "Is it a quiet and strong animal?'' he asked. "We have to take a very long journey in a day or two, and as you can see, my wife will need a quiet and strong animal to carry her. We have to go all the way from here to Jerusalem.''

"Quiet?" exclaimed Jonah, "and strong?" And he began counting off all the possible virtues a donkey could have, and wound up by saying how they were all contained in this one animal. The little donkey stood there with his head demurely hanging down, its smooth coat glistening in the sun, as though it were listening to every word and believed them all. "This animal," Jonah concluded, "is the steadiest, quietest creature you could find anywhere."

"How much is it?" asked Joseph, getting ready to add, as he had done so many times that afternoon, that it was too dear for him.

"Two pieces of silver," said Jonah, "that's all, just two pieces of silver."

"What!" exclaimed Joseph, and he and Mary looked at each other hardly able to believe their ears. "Only two pieces? But are you sure it is all you say it is?" Whereupon Jonah threw his arms into the air, and called heaven to witness that every word he said was true, and asked that all sorts of disasters might fall on him if there were only one word of untruth in it all.

And so Joseph was persuaded to buy it, and he handed over the two pieces of silver to Jonah.

Meanwhile, Mary was not only still stroking the donkey's neck and ears, but was talking to it as people do, and was telling it all about the journey they had to make, and how they expected it to be a very good donkey. And the donkey not only stood there as though it understood every word, but as though nothing less than the most perfect behavior were to be expected from it.

"D'you know, Joseph," she said, when the purchase was completed, "I really believe there is something special about this donkey. I am sure that somehow it was brought here so that we might buy it and go to Jerusalem with it. Would you help me, because I think instead of leading it I'd like to get used to it straight away by riding it home."

At these words a look of alarm spread over Jonah's face, and gathering his robe about him, he was just on the point of making himself scarce as quickly as he could when what he saw made him stand there as if turned to stone. His mouth gaped open, and astonishment was written in every line of his roguish face; for with a hand from Joseph to help her, Mary got up upon the donkey, which stood there like a rock without even twitching so much as an ear until she was comfortably seated. Then, at a word from Joseph, it began to walk away, picking its path over the rough, rocky ground as though it were watching out for every little stone that might cause it to sway or stumble; and Mary sat there like the Queen of Heaven she was, riding on the noblest beast of all the four-footed race.

Jonah could not believe his eyes. Could this be the same beast, the one which could not endure a straw on its back without kicking up its heels like a wild thing? And he had let it go for just two pieces of silver!

"What a fool I've been," he said to himself. "I could have asked twice the sum," and as he stared at those two pieces of silver in his hand a wicked idea came into his head. "I'll soon make up for that," he said and, taking a short cut between the stalls and half running to cut them off, he made his way quickly from the market to intercept Mary and Joseph just as they were leaving.

"Hey, stop!" he called out. "You haven't paid me enough. I said four pieces of silver, and you've only given me two. I didn't notice it at the time, watching you ride away so satisfied; but when I saw what was in my hand I had to come and get the rest. You couldn't have heard me properly."

Joseph just looked at him in amazement. "Four!" he exclaimed, "You distinctly said only two."

"No, four," shouted Jonah. "You don't think I'd sell a beautiful donkey like that for two, do you?" And turning to the crowd—for somehow there is always a crowd when two people start an argument about money—he asked everybody and nobody in particular, "Who would sell a beautiful beast like this for just two miserable pieces of silver?" Soon the two of them began arguing for all they were worth, while Mary still sat on the donkey, wondering what the end of it all was going to be.

"All right, then" said Jonah at length. "If you really think anybody but a fool would sell a donkey like that for two miserable pieces of silver, come back with me to the market judge, and let him settle it."

Now the market judge was just what those words mean. In the markets in those days, and in that part of the world, there were always these arguments about the price of things; and as people could get very hot tempered, and sometimes even violent about it, each market had a judge to whom these differences could be brought. What he decided was final. So they all presented themselves before the judge who sat on a kind of raised up bench in the middle of the market place; and Jonah stated his case, making as much of it as he could.

"Just look at that animal," he said to the judge; and as it stood there with Mary still on its back, it really was a beautiful creature to look at. "The king of all the donkeys that ever were. Who would be such a fool as to sell an animal like that for only two pieces of silver? Why, the four that I asked for was less than I ought to have asked; but I could see that they were poor, and so I took pity on them and decided to let them have it for four. But two!" And he spat with contempt at the thought that he could ever have asked so little.

Meanwhile the judge was quietly studying both the donkey and Jonah. "You say you sold this donkey as a quiet, easily-managed animal?" he asked.

"Yes," said Jonah, "there isn't a quieter, more gentle beast in all the world. I myself have ridden it hundreds of times over all sorts of roads, and it has never once caused me to tremble or shake."

Now the moment he said that the judge knew he was lying. Unknown to Jonah, the judge had happened to pass his house one day just after the donkey had thrown Jonah. Jonah had not seen the judge; he was too busy beating and cursing the donkey. But the judge had seen him; and he determined now to give him a lesson. "In that case," the judge said, "I would like you to get on its back yourself, and to show us how quiet it is. Ride it a little way up and down here in front of us."

You should have seen Jonah's face. He looked helplessly first at the judge, and then at the people standing around. But it was obvious that they all thought that was the fairest thing to do. "What, here in the market?" Jonah asked, desperately trying to think up a good excuse for not doing so. "You know, my rheumatism bothers me very much these days, and I'm afraid . . . "

"I don't think that matters, if the donkey is as quiet as you say," insisted the judge. "Someone will help you up."

Mary slid off the donkey as Jonah approached full of anxiety. Laying his hands on the donkey's back, he looked round once more at the judge, but there was no relenting there."Just up and down a few yards," the judge said, "so that we can all see how quiet it is."

By now quite a crowd had gathered round, and there were several there who knew Jonah and the donkey. They were all agog to see what would happen. But to their astonishment, and even more to Jonah's, the donkey stood quite still while he clambered on its back, fearful every moment of what might happen. But the donkey remained quite still. Even then Jonah hesitated to give the word to move on; but eventually he had to, and the donkey moved off as daintily as a fine stepping horse.

When Jonah recovered from his surprise, he was overjoyed at how easily he was proving his case. For once the donkey was being really useful to him. He went up and down more times than he needed to; and as he was coming past the judge the last time, he looked him triumphantly in the face, and said, "There you are, your honor. You can see that . . ."

But he never finished that sentence.

At that moment the donkey had just got to where there was a great pile of dirty, messy rubbish—one of those heaps which all markets have—where all the rotten, filthy garbage of the market is thrown. What happened next happened so quickly that no one really saw it properly. But suddenly, without the slightest warning, the little donkey arched its back, flung up its heels and, with perfect aim, deposited Jonah right in the middle of that heap of rubbish. And then having done so, it stood quite still with its head demurely lowered as if it had been standing there like that all day long.

While the crowd roared with laughter, the judge himself joining in, Jonah picked himself up. Covered in all the filth of the market place, and definitely the loser in his argument, he had the sense to creep away as quickly as he could.

"I think that proves the donkey is not so gentle as the man claimed," said the judge to Joseph, "and if you still want it for the two pieces of silver you paid, then the donkey is yours."

So Mary once more got on the donkey's back, and Joseph led the two of them out of the market place.

And that was the donkey that carried Mary all the way from Nazareth to Bethlehem where Jesus was born, and carried her without a jolt or shake in all that long, difficult journey.

What became of the donkey afterward no one really knows; but many years later when Jesus was a grown man, and himself had to ride into Jerusalem one day, he too rode on a donkey. It was not this donkey, of course; but someone (nobody knows who) left a donkey for him outside his house, and all Jesus had to do, when he was ready, was to send somebody to fetch it. I do not know of course; but I would not be a bit surprised if it were not a descendant of this same donkey that carried his mother to Bethlehem just before he was born. After all, you don't find donkeys like that just anywhere.

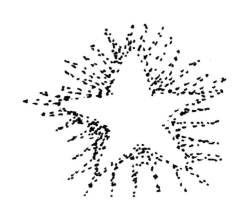

THE STAFF

THE STAFF

When Joseph and Mary went on the long journey from Nazareth to Jerusalem, they had to go on foot, of course. Mary rode on the donkey, and Joseph took a staff with him to help him along the way. It was not his staff, and yet neither was it anyone else's. It was just an ordinary stick which somebody had cut out of a tree, and which had been standing in the corner of his workshop ever since he first went to Nazareth. Whether it had belonged to the last owner of the shop or someone else he did not know.

Joseph had never used it. Although he was getting on in years now, and although the ways in the country round about Nazareth were quite rough, he liked to believe that he could still do without a staff like a young man. But this journey to Jerusalem was another matter. It would not only take them many days; but from what Joseph had heard, the way in some places was very, very bad. Besides, you never knew what might happen on a journey like this, and to have a good, stout staff in your hand might be something to be grateful for if there should be any difficulties.

"I wonder whose it was," he said as he took it up from the corner and examined it. It was quite smooth to the touch, with that smoothness that only constant use by a human hand could give it, but it was as hard as iron, too. Carpenter though Joseph was, he could not for the life of him tell what kind of wood it was, nor what tree it had come from; nor could any one else. He had once asked an old man about it who had come into his shop. "Never seen any wood like that hereabout," the old man said; "might be the staff Adam walked out of Paradise with, for all I know—or anybody else for that matter!" And although Joseph had smiled at the old man's remark at the time, it came back to him again and again after he got back from Jerusalem.

Just now he was only too pleased that it was a good stout stick he could use, without having the trouble of cutting one himself.

So, a day or two later, off they went; Mary riding on the little donkey, and Joseph walking with his staff beside her holding the donkey's bridle. They took the journey very steadily, and as they went along they talked of this and that, or just remained silent as the mood took them. But before they had gone very far, they had something to talk about which they returned to again and again. And the subject was none other than this same staff Joseph was walking with.

It began to show remarkable properties!

Joseph first noticed it after they had been walking for several hours one day and, feeling tired, he decided to stop and to have a rest. So letting go of the donkey's bridle, he just leaned on his staff for a few moments, clasping it tightly with both hands and letting his chin rest on the top.

Almost immediately he began to notice the strangest thing. Starting with his fingers, he began to feel something like a gentle, warm glow spread slowly up his arms and then across his shoulders and down through his body and legs, until it reached the very tips of his toes. It was the most refreshing sensation he had ever felt. All his tiredness seemed to ooze out of him. He felt as if he had just woke up out of a good night's sleep, fresh and eager for a hard day's work.

"I think we'll push on after all, Mary," he said, and taking hold of the donkey's bridle, he began to lead it forward again.

"But you have hardly rested at all, Joseph, really," Mary said, looking at him anxiously, wondering whether he was just pushing on in spite of himself. "You surely have time to rest longer than that before going any further."

"I don't think I was so tired after all," replied Joseph cheerfully. "In any case, I am all right now, so don't worry." And he strode forward like a young man, while Mary continued to cast anxious glances in his direction.

Saying nothing for some time to Mary about the strange sensation, Joseph found some excuse to stop every now and then for a moment to lean against his staff. He clasped it in both hands, and each time he did, the same thing happened.

At length, he could keep silent no longer, so he stopped and told Mary all about it. She was as amazed and interested as he was. In fact, she slipped off the donkey's back and tried it for herself. And, of course, it was the same for her, too.

"What can it be, Joseph?" she asked.

"I don't know any more than you, my dear," he replied, "except that it must be something to do with this staff. I thought there was something unusual about it when I first picked it up, but I never imagined anything like this. Anyway, whatever it is, it is something to thank God for, so let's be getting on our way."

And so they did. But you may depend upon it that as they trudged along, there was hardly anything else either of them thought about or spoke about. In fact, it was thinking and talking about the staff so much that drew Joseph's attention to something else that he had not noticed before; the staff was actually guiding him along the road!

Now, I do not mean that Joseph was walking along with his eyes shut, or that he was not bothering to look where he was going. But nonetheless he found that every time he put his foot down it always landed on the firmest, smoothest place of the rough road, whether he were looking down or not.

And that was something remarkable on those roads! They were not roads as we know them; but just tracks covered with loose stones, and with holes and ruts all over the place. If you did not watch your step, you could easily turn your ankle. Indeed, it was just because of the state of the roads that Joseph had brought a staff in the first place. It was a kind of extra leg to support him if one of his own slipped or stumbled.

And how easy it was to do that he soon found when he tried carrying the staff without using it. Then he often stumbled; but the moment he began using the staff properly again, he walked along as firmly as if the road were perfectly smooth.

Of course, this made quite a difference to the rate at which they travelled. It meant that every day they arrived in good time at the place they had decided to rest for the night; and both of them, particularly Mary, was able to get a good night's sleep before they continued their journey the next day.

Except the day they lost their ox!

Now you know already that besides Joseph, Mary and the donkey they had an ox with them—Joseph's ox, of course. And the idea was that as soon as they got to Jerusalem, he would sell it to pay the taxes to the King's officers. Well, this ox was walking along with them, too, fastened by a rope round its neck which was tied to the donkey's saddle. There was no need to bother about it because it just followed patiently behind; and wherever they stopped to rest or to eat, Joseph untied it and let it graze by the side of the road. But on this particular day when he fastened it to the donkey, he could not have tied the knot very firmly; for when he looked round to see if all was in order, the ox was not there.

"Now, what's happened to that ox?" he exclaimed. Although they stopped and looked all round, they could not see a sign of it anywhere.

"Oh, dear," said Joseph, "it must have got loose. We shall just have to go back and find out what's happened to it." And turning the donkey round they started retracing their steps. They found it, of course, about a mile or two farther back, quietly grazing at the side of the road with the loose rope dangling from its neck. But by the time they got back to where they first missed it, it was already getting late. The sun was beginning to go down, and there was no possibility that they would be able to make that night's resting place before dark.

However, that was the least of their worries; for now they were approaching a part of the road that was known far and wide as the Valley of Dread!

It was so named because it was said to be the resort of wild bands of robbers who terrorized the country thereabout. These men would stop at nothing, and they did not hesitate to kill their victims if they showed the slightest resistance. Very few of them were ever caught, because there were all sorts of places in this wild country among the rocks where they could hide out, moving from one side to the other if any attempt was made to hunt for them. Few travelers liked going through this valley even by day, and no one who knew anything about it at all would dare to go through it at night. And yet this was what Joseph and Mary now had to do.

Chief among the robbers who had their haunts there was one named Barabbas. He was a young man then; but years later, when he was no longer young, he actually owed his life to Jesus, who at this time was the unborn baby Mary was carrying within her. He had no idea of that, of course, and it is doubtful if he ever knew, later, to whom he really owed his life when he lay in prison at that time awaiting death. All he thought about was robbery, and he had no mercy for man, woman, or child if either came between him and his desire.

And it was through such a valley where Barabbas was known to be that Joseph and Mary had to pass. There was no other way around; and as they descended into it, they walked along without saying a word, keeping a sharp look out on every side. Every rock might have a desperate robber behind it ready to spring out on them.

Nothing happened to them, however, until they rounded a bend in the road, and then quite suddenly evil-looking men appeared in front of them and behind them, blocking their way both forward and back. The two were helpless, trapped!

While Mary sat still on her donkey, silently breathing a prayer, one of the men—quite a young man by the look of him—stepped forward. As he approached, Joseph said to himself, "This must be none other than the terrible Barabbas himself."

"Give us everything you've got," said the man; "that ox, the donkey the woman is riding on, and any money. If you try to stop us, we'll kill you and take it anyway."

Now apart from the ox and the donkey, there was very little else that Joseph had to give; but without the ox and the donkey, what would they do? It was impossible for Mary to walk the rest of the way to Jerusalem; and if he did not have the ox to sell when he got there, how was he to pay his taxes? That would mean prison, at least, and no one could tell when he would get out of there. He thought of pleading with the robbers, but he could see that was hopeless. So in utter helplessness he just leaned on his staff, clasping it with both hands, wondering what to do.

But he did not have to wonder long. As he leaned on his staff, he not only felt that same surge of revival, but this time strength, too, and courage! It amazed him how strong and brave he felt. It was no ordinary strength either; it was like the strength of ten men—of a hundred even. He suddenly felt that he could face a whole army of robbers on his own. He was like Samson, that hero of old, who had struck down the Philistines by the score with only the jawbone of an ass in his hand. So, taking up a position of defense, Joseph dared those robbers to do their worst.

Oh, how they laughed to see him—that elderly man standing there in the middle of the road with nothing but a stick to protect himself from armed cutthroats. This was something they would talk and laugh about for days to come. They did not even bother to move at first. They just waited to see what their leader would do; and he with proud insolence strolled leisurely toward Joseph, and with a quick movement grasped the staff to twist it out of his hand.

But that was all he ever did; and even then he did not so much as grasp it, for as soon as his fingers only touched the staff he let out the most unearthly yell and was flung headlong to the ground, just as if a giant had picked him up and thrown him there.

The others stared in amazement. Surely this could not be! But there indeed was their leader, senseless on the ground; and that simple old man had not as much as aimed a blow at him.

As they recovered one by one from the shock of it all they began, very tentatively, however, to creep up on Joseph to take his staff from him. One or two of them even managed to touch it, but that was all. With the same terrible cry, they were flung into the air and thrown headlong to the ground.

Presently those that were left, seeing what was happening to their companions, withdrew as quickly as they could. Whatever this was, it was more than they wanted to have a part in. Soon Joseph was left there as puzzled as anyone, still grasping his staff and looking at the recumbent bodies lying on the ground.

Presently, the leader, Barabbas, began to stir. Very slowly he raised himself into a sitting position; but then only to stare, his face white with terror, at something above and behind Joseph. Joseph himself could not resist following the robber's gaze; and turning saw behind him, reaching it seemed almost to the sky, a majestic, heavenly figure, glowing with radiant light, and with great wings outspread enclosing Mary and himself. And the look on the angel's face! . . . No wonder Barabbas was so terrified.

Joseph had often heard the phrase "the wrath of God"; he had often seen the wrath of man, too; but never in all his life had he seen, nor could he have imagined, a look of wrath like that which shone on the face of the angel.

Then the angel, looking directly at Barabbas, spoke. "Get on thy feet thou evil man, Barabbas," the angel commanded; and Barabbas, this fearless terrible robber, obeyed like a cowed animal or slave.

"Know, Barabbas, that thy evil doings have come up before God, and He Himself hath sent me this night lest thou do a deed that neither man nor God would forgive for all eternity. Go! Take the bridle of the ass on which this holy woman rides, and do thou thyself lead them in safety out of this evil place. If the slightest harm should come upon them, remember thou shalt one day answer for it before God, as thou must already answer for thy evil ways before man."

Without a word, Barabbas rose and did exactly as the angel commanded. Like the humblest slave he took the bridle of the donkey and, with Joseph following behind led them on their way down through the Valley of Dread.

It is hardly necessary to say, therefore, that they came through quite safely. Whether other robbers were on the look out for travelers like Joseph and Mary, and quickly changed their minds when they saw who was accompanying them I can not say; or whether the Angel was also following behind them. Certainly none were seen.

When they were at last out of the valley and safely on the road that led to Bethlehem, Barabbas stopped. Handing the bridle to Joseph, he said no more than, "There will be no danger now," and with one terrifying look at Joseph's staff, he slipped away into the darkness as if he could not get away quickly enough; and neither of them saw him any more. And so Mary and Joseph came at length to Bethlehem and there, as you know, Mary's child Jesus was born.

Joseph never told anyone else about that staff. When he got back to Nazareth, he put it again in the corner of his workshop where he had first found it, and there it remained as long as he lived. When, after a long life, Joseph at length died and went back to that country from which we all come, that staff disappeared, too. Where it went, who took it, no one knows; but it was never seen or heard of again.

So, perhaps what the old man had said earlier was truer than he knew, and whether it was the staff Adam had taken with him from Paradise or not, it must have come from a tree that does not grow on any earthly soil.

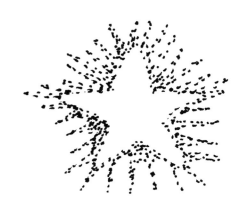

THE STRAW

THE STRAW

Many strange and wonderful things happened on the night when Jesus was born in Bethlehem, but perhaps the strangest and most wonderful was what happened to a man named Judas who was living there. Judas was a rich man, the richest in all the country roundabout perhaps, but nobody knew how rich he was for the simple reason that he never let anyone guess. He pretended by the way he lived to be very, very poor. In short, he was what we would today call a miser. He loved money, the look of it, the feel of it, even the thought of it as he counted out and let the beautiful gold and silver coins slip through his fingers. Doting over his money was his greatest joy in life.

He kept it all in a wooden box which he hid in a hole in the ground inside his house. He covered the hole with a piece of wood like a trap door, over that he laid a piece of old carpet, and over that again he placed his rough table. And there for the most part his money stayed, except on those nights when he took it out to count it.

And that was what he was doing on the night when Jesus was born.

Not that he knew what was happening, or even cared. There was only one thing in the whole world that Judas ever bothered about, and that was his money.

So after he made sure that no one was likely to disturb him, he pushed back his table, lifted up the piece of carpet, uncovered the hole, and took out his box of money. Setting it on the table, he opened it and smiled with delight at all that lay therein, when suddenly a knock came at the door.

Now who on earth could that be? People rarely knocked on Judas's door during the day; and as for nighttime, he could not remember when anyone had last come at that hour. It disturbed him; and his anxiety became worse when he remembered that he had not put the stout wooden bar across the door as was his usual custom every night. Suppose they should knock again and, not hearing a reply, come in and find him there with all that money. That was to be prevented at all costs.

So hastily snatching up a light he made his way to the door; and what was his relief when he found on opening it only one of the serving maids from the inn a few yards up the road. But that did not prevent him from showing his resentment at being disturbed.

"What do you want?" he asked indignantly. "Why do you

come bothering me at this time of night?''

But the girl was not to be put off by his surliness. It was not for nothing that she had come to his door. "Oh, Judas," she exclaimed, "would you let me have some straw, please? There is a poor woman up at the inn who has just come all the way from Nazareth with her husband to pay their taxes, and my master had nowhere to put them but in the stable. They didn't mind that; but since then she has given birth to a baby—and what a wonderful baby—but the only place we have to put the baby is in the manger; and we can't even do that yet because we haven't anything soft for him to lie on. We need some straw. So please let me have some, just enough to fill a manger.''

"Straw!" exclaimed Judas; "I haven't any straw.''

That was a lie, of course. He had a whole shed full of it at the back of his house; but he neither wanted to give any of it away (yes, he was as mean as that) nor did he want the trouble of fetching it, particularly with his treasure lying open on the table. Anybody could come in and take it while he was doing so.

"Go away and leave me in peace! It is nothing to me when babies are born, or where they are born. Get off with you!''

The girl would have been only too pleased to do so. Nobody liked asking Judas for anything, and she herself was no exception; but the matter was urgent, and Judas so close at hand.

"I will," she replied; "but please give me a bit of straw first.

Just enough to put in the manger for the little thing to lie on, so that his mother can have some rest."

"I tell you I haven't got any," he shouted at her. Raising his arm, he threatened to drive her away by force if she did not go at once. So the girl ran off as quickly as she could to try somewhere else.

Meanwhile, Judas was just about to close the door when he saw a stranger standing where the girl had stood; and this stranger was looking at him with a very penetrating, reproachful look. Judas was so surprised that for a moment he could almost have believed that the girl had changed herself into this man. He had not seen or heard him come; and he could not have been there before the girl ran off, or she would have bumped into him. He seemed to have just materialized out of the shadows.

Judas wanted to slam his door in the stranger's face, but there was something about the man's look that not only made him think better of it, but he suddenly realized he had no power in his limbs to do so. A strange feeling of awe and fear came over him, as though he were in the presence of a being from another world. He wanted desperately to say, in his usual gruff manner, "What do you want?" but the words just would not come, any more than his arms and legs would move to close the door.

"And you would not give a mere handful of straw to help a poor newborn child lie softly this night," the stranger said at length; emphasizing each word so that Judas felt the full weight of his meanness and—to his credit, let it be said—felt also a tinge of shame at it. "How mean can you get, Judas, you with all your wealth.''

The mention of his name, and more particularly his wealth, startled Judas. Who was this stranger? Judas had never seen him before, and he dared not ask. He had the feeling that he was standing before a judge, and not just an earthly judge, but a judge of all mankind. He had often heard of the judgment day that was supposed to come after this life was over, but he had never believed it, nor bothered very much about it. But now he began to feel differently. He even wondered if, in some strange way, it was already happening; for he could see all his own mean, miserly life mirrored in the penetrating gaze of this stranger, who had meanwhile neither moved nor taken his eyes off him.

"It must go hard with you, Judas," the stranger went on, "if you do not learn before you die that all your wealth is no better than straw in the eyes of God. The only wealth that any man has is what he gives away to those in need." And with that he disappeared, as mysteriously as he had come; and Judas stood there staring out into the darkness like one in a trance, while those last words reechoed in his mind.

In a moment or two, however, he had snapped out of it and, muttering to himself, "I must be dreaming," the thought of what he had been doing before all this happened came back to him. So dismissing it all from his mind, he shut and barred his door and made his way back to his room.

Imagine, then, his amazement when he got there and, going

straight to his box, he found that all his money had become straw. Yes, everything else was there just as he had left it, with the box standing open on the table; but instead of money, it was just full of straw.

He could not believe his eyes. This could not be so; he must be bewitched! Dashing forward he began pulling out the straw and throwing it aside only to discover there was no money there at all—not a single piece. As the last bit of straw dropped from his hand, and he realized that all the money was gone, he sank stupified to the ground.

For a long time he just sat there like someone out of his mind, not speaking, not even thinking, just staring stupidly at that empty box, which only a few moments before contained all the wealth he had gathered through a long life of scrimping and saving, and of buying cheap and selling dear—not to mention quite a bit of lying and cheating, too. Now it was all gone—all of it—and nothing remained but straw.

Straw?

"Why, of course," he cried, as a sudden idea broke on his dazed mind and, jumping up from the ground, he exclaimed, "That's it! I've been robbed! All that about the straw was a trick. While I was talking to her at the front, there were others who came around the back and stole my money." And without a thought of who they could have been, and how they could have got in, and why after stealing his money they should take the trouble to fill it up with straw, he yelled, "But they shan't get away with it"; and, leaving everything just as it was, he dashed away to the inn to find them.

He had only a few steps to go. When he got there, it was all closed up and dark. But at the side where the stable was, there was a light shining beneath the door.

"That's where they are," he said to himself. "They are in there, probably already sharing out my money among them. Now I'll be able to catch them in the very act," and creeping up to the door, he waited for a few moments and then he suddenly flung it open.

For a moment the light that poured out almost blinded him, so he had to stand there until he got used to it. When he did, instead of robbers, all he saw was a young woman in a blue gown holding a little child, from whom all this light seemed to shine in a wonderful golden glow on everything around—on the mother's face as she bent over the child, on the old man as he leaned on his staff, on the ox, everything—even now on the face of Judas himself!

They did not seem a bit disturbed, though the silence and stillness of it all quite unnerved Judas. He stood there with his hand still on the door, as motionless as they, like one who has just stepped into another world.

Presently as his eyes wandered from one to the other, he found himself looking fixedly at a figure standing behind the woman and her husband. It was no earthly figure; and even Judas had heard enough about angels to know that he was now looking at an angel face to face, for the first time. No, not the first time! Only a few moments before he had looked into that same heavenly countenance when he had driven the innkeeper's serving maid empty-handed from his door.

81

A great fear fell upon Judas. He forgot all about what he had come for, all about his money. All he knew was that something was happening to him, and that if he didn't take notice of it he might just as well be dead. He looked up at the angel, hoping that the angel had something to say to him to help him, but the angel had no eyes for Judas now. The angel was looking steadfastly at something in front of the little family group, something at Judas's feet. And as Judas followed the angel's gaze his eyes, too, came to rest on an empty manger.

He needed no words, either of angel or man, to tell him what that meant. For a moment—much, much shorter than it takes me to tell you— as Judas looked into that empty manger, he once again saw his whole life come up before him. Not his past life this time, but the life he could live in the future, a life of joy and gladness with his fellow man, a life in which he could find his greatest happiness in taking part in their joy and sorrow, a life of giving and not getting, a life of fellowship and not rejection; and it all depended on what happened to that empty manger.

Now it's hard to believe that a man's life can be completely changed in a moment, especially a bad man's life; but it does happen, and it always starts with one simple thing he has to do. For Judas it all centered around that manger. He knew what he had to do; and so . . .

"Excuse me, ma'am," he heard himself saying, in a voice that was so new to him that he hardly recognized it as his own; "but wouldn't you like to rest a while. Why not put the baby to sleep in the manger? I'll get you some straw for it." And without a moment's delay he ran out and, in what seemed like no time, came running back with a great bundle of straw and some wool as well to go on top of it. In a moment he had made as comfortable a bed inside that manger as any child could need.

Then when this was done, the miracle happened. At least it was a miracle for Judas, the miracle that changed his life; and as long as he lived he never tired of talking about it. As Mary placed the child in the manger, the child's little fingers closed round just one wisp of straw that was sticking out from beneath the wool. When he was at last settled, he held out this piece of straw to Judas; and Judas of course took it. And then (though I know people will tell you that babies can not smile until several days after they are born) this baby smiled at Judas.

Whatever it was that Judas learned by that smile, whatever it was that smile ''told'' him, it must have been something very wonderful; for he was a completely changed man afterwards. He went back home with that piece of straw in his hand and sat up half the night just looking at it and thinking of all that had happened. He did not bother about his money that was scattered all over the floor where he had flung it when he had come in first; for, of course, as you have probably guessed, it was not really straw. He had only thought it was straw, for things like that can happen to people. It had been money then, and it was still money; but at the time—and the angel-stranger must have had something to do with it, for angels can do things like that if they want to—he thought it was straw. But now, whether it was money or straw or anything else, he had no eyes for it.

It was not till the next day that he noticed it at all; and then he just picked it all up and put it on one side, and before long it was gone. "How . . . gone?" did you say. Why, he just gave it away! Whenever a poor beggar came to his door, or if ever he heard of anybody in distress, he just gave it away to help them.

Before long he was the most well-known and best-loved man in all Bethlehem—although some thought he was just a little bit crazy, too. That happened whenever people spoke about treasure or riches for he could not help telling them that he was the richest man in the world; and if those who did not know his story asked him to prove it, he took them back to his house. And there, after moving his table and taking up the old bit of carpet, and then moving the wood and lifting out his treasure box, he would open it and hold up to their astonished and often disgusted gaze—one small wisp of straw.

But it really was treasure, his treasure. It had changed his whole life and had brought him a happiness that he could never have imagined before. And though it must have seemed strange, to say the least, that a man should make so much of a bit of straw; and though one can understand how some people thought him a bit crazy; I for my part think there's a lot in what one man said about it all, "If Judas is crazy, then I wish a few more people who believe themselves sensible, could be as crazy as he is."

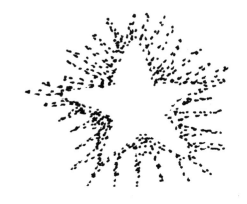

_____ Part III _____

NO ROOM

Every year, a few days before Christmas, it was old Matthew Goodyear's custom to go out into the streets of the little town where he lived looking for homeless people. When he found them he would take these people back to his house and, after giving them a good meal for the night, would invite them to stay with him over Christmas. And invariably they did. When the holiday was over he did everything he could to find them work, or he gave them the means to move on to where they wanted to go.

He was able to do this because he lived all by himself in a fairly large house, and though he was not what you would call a rich man, he was well enough off to be able to do it.

He had been doing it for years; and never had he been disappointed in his ''guests'', and never had one of them taken advantage of his hospitality. On the contrary, by the time the initial strangeness was over—and with a man like old Matthew that hardly took any time at all—they settled down to being as helpful and jolly a house party as anyone could wish. Not only was Matthew himself the most genial of hosts, but—a firm believer in the traditional Christmas—the spirit of Christmas infected his guests; and they all joined with him in making it that kind of Christmas you only read about now, or see pictured on Christmas cards.

It all started one Christmas many years before when Matthew had been reading, as was his custom, the story of the birth of Jesus in the gospel according to St. Luke; and, although he had read it often before, he had been particularly struck by the words, "and there was no room for them in the inn." He was suddenly amazed that such could have been the case.

"Surely there must have been room somewhere," he said to himself over and over again; "and if an angel of God could have come and told a few shepherds what was happening, surely one could have told somebody who had room to be prepared for them."

This really puzzled him. He was a simple man and was not given to theological arguments as a rule; but this, because it seemed so easy of solution, really perplexed him.

"Now if only all this had happened today and had happened here," he went on, "and Joseph and Mary had come to my door—I not only could, but I should have been delighted to give them room." He was a kindly disposed sort of man, and he could not believe that there were not thousands of others like him in the world.

And then the other side of it struck him.

"But what do I do, myself, now?" he asked. "There are still plenty of people who can't find a roof over their heads;" and he remembered vividly one poor fellow he had seen only that day, trudging along the road hopelessly cast down.

And that's how it all started. He went out there and then, that very night and found someone whom he brought back with him; and he vowed that he would never let another Christmas pass without filling his house with people who had nowhere else to go; and every

Christmas thereafter his house was filled with the poorest people he could find.

Now on this particular Christmas I want to tell you about (and, by the way, I should have told you that all this happened many, many years ago, when the conditions of the poor were much worse than they are now) Matthew's house was full. There was an old soldier who had been travelling about from town to town begging his living; a gypsy woman whose people had abandoned her, but who was most active and cheerful; a young man who had been travelling south looking for work; a foreign sailor who had no friends or people to help him; and a pedlar woman who had been robbed of all her little store of goods, and whom Matthew had found sitting under a hedge wondering what she should do next.

And now on Christmas Eve they had all taken part in preparing for the celebrations they were going to share the next day. Everyone was busy. The two women had shown a wonderful gift for decorating the house; the old soldier had proved himself an excellent cook; the young man had chopped and laid in wood; and the house had been cleaned from top to bottom.

After they had one by one gone off to bed, Matthew sat thinking about them all, and all they had told him about themselves. He had never realized before how interesting other people's lives were; but when the old clock chimed the hour he decided to follow them up to bed. He was just having a last look round when he was startled to hear a loud knock on the front door.

For a moment he was half inclined to let the knock go unanswered, but it was repeated, and he decided he had better see who it could be. So taking up a candle he made his way to the door.

On the doorstep he found a man who stood there looking at him wonderingly, half in fear, and half in hope. "Excuse me, master," he began, "but have you somewhere where my wife and I could pass the night. We're on our way to London, but my wife is so weary she just can't go another step. Anywhere would do as long as it is somewhere dry."

For a moment Matthew just looked at him. His heart went out to the man, and he would have liked to take them in, but...the words were out before he could think about them, and he heard himself saying, "I'm sorry, but my house is full. You'll have to try..." and it was not until long after, that he realized how very near he had come to saying the very same words he had passed judgment on in the story of Mary and Joseph.

But it was the woman, the man's wife, who not only prevented him from saying these words, but also settled the matter for him; for on hearing that there was no room for them, with a stifled cry she sank to the ground in utter weariness and exhaustion.

In a moment Matthew was a different man. "Quick!" he said to the man, "I'll give you a hand; bring her in here;" and between them they raised her to her feet and half carried, half led her into the house.

Matthew made her comfortable in a chair by the fire, heaped on more wood and blew it to a blaze, bustled about getting food and a warm drink; and then, having noticed while he was doing it the reason for her exhaustion, the fact that she was soon to give birth, he went and roused his two women guests and asked them to come and help.

Before long he had both the man and his wife comfortable, and the activity had not only brought the two women down, but the rest of Matthew's guests, in various kinds of night attire, had also, one by one, crept in to see what was going on.

But now—where was he going to put them? For though Matthew might have had a very good reason when they were on his doorstep for asking them to go elsewhere, there could be no question of turning them out now they were in. And of course such an idea did not even enter his head; but nonetheless, where was he going to put them? And as the only possible answer came to him, he went over to the pedlar woman and whispered something in her ear; and she, nodding in understanding, slipped quietly out of the room to attend to it.

Meanwhile the young couple had finished eating and were sitting there somewhat embarrassed, looking at one another, hardly able to believe their good fortune.

"I think it would be best if you went to bed now," said Matthew. "A good night's sleep is what you both need, and everything is ready for you. Don't worry about anything tonight. Tomorrow we'll talk about it, and you can stay here as long as you like." Taking a candle, and with the young woman leaning on her husband's arm, and the others doing whatever they could to help, Matthew led them up to the only room left in the house—his own!

The pedlar woman had meanwhile got everything ready, and when she and Matthew were outside the door, once again he whispered something to her with a serious look on his face. "Don't you worry,'' she said. ''I'll be able to see to it. I've had several of my own and have helped many another in my time. I'll leave my door ajar, and I've told her husband he's to come if he should need me.''

So one by one they all went back to their own rooms; and Matthew, descending to the kitchen, wondered for the first time since it had all happened, where he was going to sleep.

At first, he thought he would try the kitchen chair, but he had slept—or tried to sleep—on chairs before without much success. Then he thought of stretching himself out on the hearthrug, but that did not appeal to him either. Then where...there was no other room in the house, unless...Yes! The attic! At the top of the house was a room where he could easily make up a bed for himself, and then tomorrow he could see about making some more permanent arrangement.

So gathering up all the spare cushions and things that he could find, he carried them all up to the attic. With the help of a couple of old chairs and a stool he found there, he soon fixed himself up a bed of sorts; and after a bit of maneuvering he got himself into it and composed himself for sleep.

He had not been lying there long, however, thinking about all the things that had happened, and particularly how glad he was that he had been able to help the young couple, when his attention was drawn to a small hole in the roof just above his head.

Being a practical man who liked to keep things in good condition, his first thought was that he must do something about it and get the local builder to repair it; when, happening to shift his position ever so slightly, he found he could see a star through that hole.

"My Christmas star," he murmured happily to himself, and he began thinking of the star that had guided the shepherds to the birthplace of Jesus. Soon he was thinking of all the wonderful things that Christmas had meant for the world; and from there...but Matthew never got to what went from there, for he presently dropped off to sleep as peacefully as a child.

The next thing he knew was that he was wide awake again. How long he had slept he could not tell. It was still quite dark, except for the star which he could still see through the little hole in the roof. But to his amazement as he watched it a strange thing began to happen. The star seemed to grow. Indeed, there was no seeming about it, for the radiance of it presently filled the hole through which he had first glimpsed it. And still it grew. At length it was not a single star out there in the heavens any longer, but a blaze of light issuing from that hole and gradually filling the room where Matthew lay.

He was at first not a little unnerved by it; and as the light got brighter, he presently began to make out within it a form and face; and one such as he had never seen on Earth before.

Matthew had often wondered what the face of an angel might look like, and of course never having seen one he had no idea.

At least he had none until that moment; but now as he gazed on that radiant, shining figure of light he knew that he was in the presence of an angel. The angel did not speak, but as Matthew watched him he noticed that he was looking toward the door of his room and was pointing to it.

Matthew had no fear now, and somehow he knew what he had

to do. So getting out of his makeshift bed, he wrapped something around him and, opening the door, went down the stairs to the rooms below. At the foot of the stairs he met the pedlar woman. She was standing there as though she had been waiting for him.

"Yes," she said, even though he had not spoken; "it's happened; and it's all over now—about an hour ago— and it was so easy and so natural. The dear girl is resting now, but I expect you'd like to come in and see the baby," and opening the door of Matthew's bedroom a crack and peeping in, she presently opened it wider and beckoned him to come in.

Matthew felt as if he were in some kind of dream, and yet it was all so real. He felt as if he were taking part in something that had been enacted before; something that did not belong to any particular time or place; something that was eternal. Even his friends—strange that that word should come so easily to his mind, and yet they were his friends, friends he felt he had known for ages—who were standing around outside the room whispering and smiling together, were part of it all.

When he got into the room he already knew what he was going to see. He had seen it so many times before in his imagination and in pictures. There was the young woman—whose name strangely enough he did not even know yet—with a newborn child in her arms, and her husband standing beside her looking down at her with unspeakable love. Presently, becoming aware that they were not alone, the young couple looked up and smiled at Matthew to come nearer and look more closely; and he stepped into the room, while the others who were outside came hesitantly after him one by one, until they were all grouped round the young couple.

On an impulse that he could not resist Matthew sank to his knees, and one by one all those around him did likewise. No one spoke, but indescribable blessing and benediction seemed to fill the whole room. Presently, raising his eyes, Matthew was not at all surprised to see standing behind the mother and father, the same angelic being of light who had first appeared to him in his attic room. This angel was looking directly at Matthew, and as he looked Matthew heard a voice as if it were sounding all round him, a voice that sang, "Whensoever a child is born on Earth, I find my way again among mankind. Blessed are they who receive Me, and twice blessed are they who behold Me in their fellow man."

What happened after that Matthew could never rightly remember. He knew he must have found his way back to his attic, because that's where he found himself in the morning when he woke up. He knew, too, that the young woman's child had been born in the night, for everybody was talking about it when he got down to breakfast. However, no one said a word about what had really happened when they had all gathered round the child in the dead of night, but it was something they all knew and remembered. It was an open secret written on the face of each of them; a secret they all shared; but a secret they could not speak about, because it was more than words could properly express. It lived in their hearts and made that Christmas the most wonderful they had ever known.

When Christmas was over, one by one they went their several ways; some of them never to see or never to hear of each other again on Earth. But there were no regrets, there was no sadness. Each of them bore away with them a Christmas gift which nothing could ever spoil or diminish; a gift that gave them courage to meet what ever life was to bring to them; a gift that had its origin, as it would have its fulfillment, in a world to which we all belong even when we know it not.

95